FREIGHT TRAINS

TRAINS

Lynn M. Stone

The Rourke Corporation, Inc.
Vero Beach, Florida 32964

PHOTO CREDITS:
Cover, title page, p. 4, 10, 12, 13, 15, 17, 18 © Lynn M. Stone; p. 7, 8 © Jerry Hennen; p. 21 from East West Rail Scenes

PRODUCED BY:
East Coast Studios, Merritt Island, Florida

EDITORIAL SERVICES:
Penworthy Learning Systems

Library of Congress Cataloging-in-Publication Data

Stone, Lynn M.
    Freight trains / by Lynn M. Stone
        p. cm. — (Trains)
    Summary: Describes the history and uses of freight trains and the different types.
    ISBN 0-86593-517-3
    1. Railroads Juvenile literature. 2. Railroads—Freight cars Juvenile literature
[1. Railroads—Trains] I. Title. II. Series: Stone, Lynn M. Trains.
TF148.S86 1999
385'.34—dc21   99-13274
                                                               CIP

Printed in the USA

TABLE OF CONTENTS

FREIGHT TRAINS

Trains that haul products, or goods, are **freight** (FRAYT) trains.

Anything these trains carry is freight. Freight trains haul lumber, furniture, scrap metal, and autos. They haul grain, oil, paper, and glass. Freight trains haul coal, chemicals, and many other products.

Freight trains are an important form of transportation. Each day as many as 10,000 freight trains rumble on tracks in the United States. The longest freights may have 200 cars and be two miles (3 kilometers) long!

A Burlington Northern Santa Fe piggyback freight train roars past a highway crossing in northern Illinois.

EARLY FREIGHT TRAINS

Today we haul freight by airplane and truck as well as by train and ship. When trains first appeared in North America, in 1830, there were no airplanes or trucks. Hauling freight on railroad tracks was a huge success.

Many companies began railroads in the eastern U.S. By the early 1850s, railroads stretched from the East Coast to the Great Lakes. Cities like St. Louis and Chicago grew rapidly because of the new railroads. By 1869, the United States had rail service all the way from California on the Pacific Coast to New York on the Atlantic.

Nearly all freight trains were powered by steam locomotives until the 1940s.

The early freight cars were made of wood. But as steam locomotives improved, so did the freight cars they pulled. Steel freight cars were first used in 1896. By the late 1920s, steel had taken over.

Wooden cattle cars (center) stand on a siding in New Mexico. Railroads gladly gave up the cattle shipping business to trucks.

FREIGHT CARS

Each type of freight car is made to carry a certain kind of freight. About a dozen types are common. Some, such as boxcars and refrigerator cars, are closed. Others, like the piggyback flatcar, are open. The piggyback flatcar earned its name from carrying truck trailers on its "back." Another open car is the gondola. The open-topped hopper car has higher sides than a gondola car. Open hoppers often carry coal. Covered hoppers have steel roofs over their freight.

Double-stack container cars haul freight in huge, stacked steel boxes.

Covered hopper car protects its freight from rain, snow, and wind.

The locomotives and cars in freight trains are put together in freight yards.

Tank cars are rounded like giant bottles. They carry liquids. Center-beam cars have open sides and upright steel frames. These cars carry stacks of lumber.

Until the 1980s, the best-known car on any freight train didn't haul freight! That car was the caboose. (See cover photo.)

The caboose carried some of the train's **crew** (KROO). It also had warning lights and instruments for checking the train.

Cabooses were replaced by small electronic devices, nicknamed FRED (Flashing Rear End Device). Each freight train has a FRED on the last car. Cabooses are rare these days.

Rack cars haul up to 18 automobiles on two or three levels.

MODERN FREIGHT TRAINS

Nearly all the trains operating in North America today are freights. In fact, $95 of every $100 earned by American railroads comes from freight service. Canadian railroads earn about $80 of every $100 from freight.

Once upon a time, railroads hauled most of the nation's freight. In 1929 the railroads owned over 2,600,000 freight cars. They hauled over 36,000,000 carloads of freight.

Truck trailers ride on a westbound freight from Chicago.

But that was before fast interstate highways and big trucks. Today the American railroads have about 1,300,000 freight cars that haul about 25,000,000 carloads of freight a year.

A popular type of freight service puts trucks and trains together. This type is called **intermodal** (in ter MO dl) freight. It links two **modes** (MODZ), or kinds, of transportation.

Piggybacks are intermodal freights. They transport truck trailers on railroad flatcars. Some intermodal freights carry large containers first hauled by ship.

A Burlington Northern mixed freight crosses a trestle near Glacier National Park, Montana.

UNIT AND MIXED FREIGHTS

Intermodal trains are one of three kinds of freight trains. Unit freight trains are made up of cars that are all alike or are all going to the same place. The whole train is one unit.

Mixed freight trains are made up of different kinds of cars bound for different places.

Already old when this photo was taken, a pair of classic General Motors F7 diesels haul mixed freight across Minnesota in 1974.

FREIGHT LOCOMOTIVES

The first freight locomotives in North America were steam powered. Freight trains were pulled or pushed mostly by steam locomotives until 1940. By then, the first diesel-electric locomotives had begun service.

Diesel-electrics were cheaper to run and service than steam engines. By 1960, diesel-electrics had replaced nearly all the steam locomotives in North America.

Nearly all modern locomotives are diesel-electric. The smaller locomotives are used in rail **yards** (YAHRDZ). Yards have many short tracks where freight cars can be stored and moved about.

GLOSSARY

crew (KROO) — people who operate a train, usually a conductor and engineer

freight (FRAYT) — goods and products transported by shippers, such as railroads

intermodal (in ter MO dl) — mixing of two methods (modes) of transportation, such as trucks and trains

mode (MOD) — a way or method of transporting goods, such as railroads

yard (YAHRD) — the place where a railroad moves, sorts, stores, and repairs hundreds of train cars

INDEX

FURTHER READING

Find out more about trains with these helpful books and information sites:
Riley, C.J. *The Encyclopedia of Trains and Locomotives.* Metro Books, 1995

Association of American Railroads online at www.aar.org
California State Railroad Museum online at www.csrmf.org
Union Pacific Railroad online at http://www.uprr.com